—— joy redefined ——
LOVING YOURSELF

D1537047

Joyce Meyer Ministries
P.O. Box 655
Fenton, Missouri 63026
joycemeyer.org

LOVING YOURSELF & LOVING YOUR LIFE

It seems that in today's society, insecurity is an epidemic. Many people lack confidence, are fearful, and they feel bad about themselves. The result is that many people don't like themselves, and this is a problem because self-rejection and self-hatred cause many relationship issues.

But this isn't the life God wants us to have.

When Jesus died on the cross, He paid the price for our sins to be forgiven so we could become ***a new creature [reborn and renewed by the Holy Spirit]*** (2 Corinthians

5:17). This means that in Christ, we can be confident, bold, fearless and free of the guilt, shame and insecurity that cause us to have an unhealthy self-image, which steals the joy out of life.

God desires for you to know who you are in Christ and to feel good about yourself. He wants you to like yourself and trust His love for you and acceptance of you.

That's why I wrote this book. I want to share my own struggle in this area and help you learn how to be at peace with God, yourself and your current circumstances. Because when you can see yourself the way God sees you, you can *have and enjoy life*—the life Jesus died to give you!

THE THIEF COMES
ONLY IN ORDER TO
STEAL AND KILL
AND DESTROY. I
CAME THAT THEY
MAY HAVE . . .

AND ENJOY LIFE,
AND HAVE IT IN
ABUNDANCE [TO
THE FULL, TILL IT
OVERFLOWS].

—JOHN 10:10

CHAPTER ONE

Finding Freedom to Love Yourself

We all have a deep need to feel good about ourselves. And we can spend a lot of time and energy trying to do things that make us feel like we're okay—okay with ourselves, with others and even God. But we don't need to wear ourselves out trying to be right with God through our own effort. The truth is, we can't make our lives right on our own, but we *can* receive the righteousness of God by putting our faith in Christ.

I spent many years of my life not liking myself. I was sexually abused by my dad throughout my childhood, and it caused me to have a root of shame in my soul. I was ashamed of who I was because I didn't understand that the way he treated me was *not* my fault, and I thought something was wrong with me.

> *Shame became a poison in my soul, and it affected the way I looked at everything and everyone else in my life.*

I compared myself to others and tried to be like them. I tried to be steady and easy-going like my husband, Dave. Then I tried to be like my pastor's wife—she was super sweet and sensitive to others. At one time, I even tried to be like my neighbor, who gardened and sewed clothes for her family.

All of this just made me more frustrated because God wasn't going to help me be anyone but myself. He wanted me to be free to become everything that He had created me to be!

Throughout my years of ministry, I have discovered that most people really don't like themselves. Some know it, while others don't even have a clue it's the root of many problems in their life.

So I want to ask you: How do you feel about yourself? I believe most people think about their relationships with others, but they don't realize they have one with themselves. We need to think about it because we have a more active relationship with ourselves than we do with anyone else.

Think about it: You never get away from yourself; everywhere you go, there you are!

*Every second of your life, you are
with YOU, and if you don't like yourself,
you're in for a miserable life.*

The good news is, God wants us to have great relationships with Him, with other people, and with ourselves. And I have found the Bible to be a book about relationships.

THE NEGATIVE CYCLE OF COMPARISON AND IMITATION

It's easy in a success-driven society to feel like we just don't quite measure up. Most people compare themselves to other people who seem to have it all together. But chances are they have some of the same problems we do.

When we compare ourselves with people, we often try to be like them. It would probably surprise you to know there are some who are looking at you, trying to be like you.

All of us have strengths and weaknesses, and we make a big mistake when we concentrate on our weaknesses.

Obviously, God wants to work with us to help us overcome moral weaknesses and attitude problems. But when it comes to the gifts and talents He's given us—those things we're able to do to serve God and help others—it doesn't do us one bit of good to continually focus on our weaknesses, trying to fix them.

For example, there was a time in my life when I was jealous of an acquaintance who played the guitar and led worship. She was also Miss Arts and Crafts and Susie Homemaker. I was nothing like her, but I decided I wanted to try to do some of the things she did. One of the things I tried to do was learn to play the guitar. The problem was, I almost failed music in school, and I have little, short fingers; I could not get them around the neck of the guitar. So I spent my time trying to learn how to play the guitar because I didn't want to just teach God's Word—I wanted to sing *and* teach.

A lot of people are like that. They're not satisfied with what they can do, so they're always trying to do something that doesn't match their skills. Maybe, if I had worked hard enough and long enough, I could have finally become a mediocre guitar player, but the world doesn't need more mediocre musicians.

Thankfully, I figured out that it was best for

me to focus on developing the natural gifting God gave me to speak and teach His Word. Over the years, as I've committed myself to studying the Word and teaching others how to apply biblical principles to their lives, I've grown and thrived in using this gift.

All of us can be excellent at something if we will just focus on and develop the skills we're naturally gifted to do. But instead, we have a tendency to look at our weaknesses, compare ourselves to others, and think that because we can't do what they can do, something's wrong with us. Then we work really hard to develop a skill or talent God never wanted us to use in the first place.

When I was trying to be like my neighbor, who was great at gardening and sewing, I felt pressured to be like "regular women" who were great housewives. The world projects an image of what one is, and it changes over time, but few of us fit into it. I've never been exactly like anybody else. And the truth is, neither have you; we're all uniquely created by God, and He has special plans and purposes for everyone.

All of us have different personalities.

We have different spiritual gifts. People have different interests and preferences. Some people love to grow gardens and sew. Others would rather eat out and buy their clothes.

We need to understand that just because we don't all like the same things, it doesn't mean there's something wrong with us. Being able to fully understand this truly sets us free to be who we were created to be.

ALL OF US CAN
BE EXCELLENT AT
SOMETHING . . .

IF WE WILL JUST

FOCUS ON AND

Many times, we try to put people in boxes that we think define them, but I want people to break out of them. In Christ, we can be free to pursue God's plans and fulfill His expectations, rather than live with the pressure to do what society says we should do.

Maybe you've been stuck in a box someone else made for you, trying so hard to be something you're not. You don't have any joy, and you don't feel fulfilled. But you've never had the confidence or the boldness to just say, "You know what? That's not me, and I'm not going to try to be something I'm not. I am going to find out what God has for me, and I am going to do it with all of my heart."

If that's where you are today, I want to encourage you to know there is a way out of the box. You can find the grace, strength and wisdom, through your relationship with Christ, to start taking steps in the right direction and discover the freedom to be YOU.

LOVING YOURSELF IS GOD'S COMMAND

In Matthew 22:36, someone asks Jesus, *"Teacher, which is the greatest commandment in the Law?"* In verses 37-38, Jesus replies, *. . . "'You shall love the Lord your God with all your heart, and with all your soul, and with all your mind.' This is the first and greatest commandment."*

Loving God is the first and the most important thing we have to do.

In verse 39, He goes on to say, **"The second is like it, 'You shall love your neighbor as yourself [that is, unselfishly seek the best or higher good for others].'"**

If you don't love yourself, then you're not going to be able to love anyone else. If you don't get along with you, you're not going to get along with anyone else. If you don't have a good relationship with yourself, you are not going to have good relationships with the other people in your life.

The greatest gift you can give to the world is a healthy you—physically, mentally and emotionally.

When people don't like themselves, I believe it's the equivalent of being emotionally ill. It's not how God wants us to function in our life. We're not supposed to have negative feelings about ourselves. We have to aggressively deal with insecurity and feelings of guilt and shame, because all they do is make us feel bad about ourselves. And if we feel insecure and inadequate, we can't love others with the love of God because we don't love ourselves.

If you have ever heard me teach, you know I don't just give people "dessert messages" that encourage them but don't challenge them to mature spiritually. I am called to give people strong teachings based on biblical principles that help them understand how God wants them to live, and they often bring correction to people's lives.

But when they leave the auditorium, they usually feel better than they did when they came in because they are empowered by the Holy Spirit through the truth they've discovered to move forward and experience more of what God has for them. Teaching from God's Word that is inspired by the Holy Spirit will not leave you feeling hopeless or that you'll never amount to anything. Truth spoken in love will always encourage you to make progress in your walk with God so you can "love your neighbor as you love yourself."

Another important verse along these lines is 1 Peter 3:10. *"**The one who wants to enjoy life and see good days [good—whether apparent or not], must keep his tongue free from evil and his lips from speaking guile (treachery, deceit).**"*

This verse says we must avoid saying evil things, and it's evil to speak negatively about yourself. We need to be very careful about what we say about ourselves. Say what God says about you in His Word, not what other people say or what you think or feel. The enemy will lie to you and try to put thoughts in your mind that contradict what God says, and you must choose to reject those thoughts and replace them with the truth.

This is so important because you believe more of what YOU say than what anyone else says. There's a great example of this in the book of Numbers.

When some of the Israelites were sent to spy out the land of Canaan, most of them came back and said, "We can't do it. There are giants and they're going to defeat us." The Bible says that they gave a bad report, and they saw themselves as grasshoppers in their own sight (see Numbers 13:31-33).

When we talk negatively, we're speaking a bad, or an evil, report. Peter is essentially saying if we want to see good days and have a good life—even in the midst of difficult circumstances—we can choose to do so. But we have to keep our tongue *free from speaking evil.*

First Peter 3:11 goes on to say, **[We]** *must turn away from wickedness and do what is right . . . search for peace [with God, with self, with others] and pursue it eagerly [actively—not merely desiring it].*

So here we see that God wants us to . . .

- **Enjoy life and see good days**

- Turn away from wickedness
  and do what's right

- **Actively pursue peace with God,
  with ourselves, and with others**

- And love our neighbor as we
  love ourselves

As we live by the wisdom in these scriptures, we'll love ourselves in a healthy, balanced way, and then we'll be able to love our neighbor as we love ourselves!

GOD WANTS EACH
OF US TO HAVE A
DEEP, INTIMATE,
PERSONAL
RELATIONSHIP
WITH HIM . . .

SO WE CAN
ENJOY OUR
EVERYDAY LIVES.

CHAPTER TWO

God Wants You to Enjoy the Journey

When we don't receive God's love or learn how to have a healthy relationship with ourselves, we can't enjoy our daily lives.

In John 10:10, Jesus says, **The thief comes only in order to steal and kill and destroy. I came that they may have and enjoy life, and have it in abundance [to the full, till it overflows].**

When I got a revelation of this scripture, it literally changed my life! It helped me understand the truth that God wants me to enjoy my life NOW, not just when I get to heaven.

I'm very passionate about teaching this truth to others because there are so many Christians who are struggling to get through the day, and they have a "barely getting by, hanging on till Jesus comes to get me" mentality that steals the joy out of everyday life. This is NOT God's plan for us as born-again believers in Christ!

Another way people lose their joy is by constantly taking an inventory of everything they've ever done wrong, every mistake they've made, and every weakness they have. Entertaining thoughts such as, *I'm just no good. I'll never amount to anything. I'm just so blessed that God would even accept me at all…* may seem humble and "religious," but this is not God's heart for us. This mindset is dangerous because it keeps us from the life Jesus died to give us.

If you identify with this struggle, you may need to negotiate a peace treaty with yourself. For the mistakes you've made, you need to ask forgiveness. And you need to really receive God's love for you and His forgiveness of your sins.

We can have confidence that we are made right with God through Christ because 2 Corinthians 5:17 tells us...

Therefore if anyone is in Christ [that is, grafted in, joined to Him by faith in Him as Savior], he is a new creature [reborn and renewed by the Holy Spirit]; the old things [the previous moral and spiritual condition] have passed away. Behold, new things have come [because spiritual awakening brings a new life].

And verse 21 (NIV) says, **God made him who had no sin to be sin for us, so that in him we might become the righteousness of God.**

These scriptures declare that once you receive Christ as your Savior, you're a new creature. You're not that old person you used to be, and through Christ, you don't have to live like it anymore.

God wants each of us to have a deep, intimate, personal relationship with Him so we can enjoy our everyday lives. Jesus died to give us relationship with Father God, not religion. And we can have it when we truly receive God's love and forgiveness.

HOW TO RECEIVE
GOD'S FORGIVENESS

Freedom in Christ means that when we make a mistake and sincerely repent, we can move on without the burden or oppression of guilt and condemnation. We don't have to waste our time and emotional energy trying to pay for our mistakes by being miserable for a month, a week, or even a day.

When we pray, God wants us to receive His forgiveness. This means we don't have to plead with Him to forgive us because *He wants to cleanse us of our sin when we sincerely repent and ask Him to do so.*

Jesus says in John 16:24, ***. . . Ask, and you will receive, that your joy may be full*** (NKJV). So when we pray, we can humbly and confidently say, "Father, I ask You to forgive my sins. I'm sorry I made a bad choice. I know it wasn't the right thing to do. And Lord, I'm not even going to promise I won't do it again because if You don't help me, I probably will do it again. So I'm leaning on You. I'm depending on You, and I want to live a better life that is pleasing to You. Now I receive Your mercy. I receive Your grace. I receive Your forgiveness." After I pray like this, I usually get quiet for a little bit and just take it in and pray, "I receive Your love. I receive a new beginning. I receive a fresh start. Thank You, Lord."

This is so important because when I'm in a right relationship with God and a right relationship with myself, then I can have a right relationship with everybody else too. But when people carry a constant burden of guilt around all the time, they don't like themselves and they are hard to get along with.

If you've struggled with the burden of religion and you need freedom from guilt and condemnation, I want to encourage you with these scriptures:

- John 8:36 says, *So if the Son makes you free, then you are unquestionably free.*

- And 2 Corinthians 3:17 tells us, **Now the Lord is the Spirit, and where the Spirit of the Lord is, there is liberty [emancipation from bondage, true freedom].**

These promises from God are so amazing!

We don't have to be burdened by a bunch of religious rules and obligations that make us believe if we don't do them, God will be angry with us or reject us. Remember John 10:10? Jesus came so we can have abundant life—*to the full, till it overflows.* I want to say it again: God wants us to enjoy our daily journey in this life!

The bottom line is that peace with God is the foundation for peace in every other area of our lives, including our relationship with ourselves and others. Jesus is the "Prince of Peace" (see Isaiah 9:6), and we experience true peace through a personal relationship with Him.

I want to encourage you to meditate on 1 John 1:9, which says, ***If we [freely] admit that we have sinned and confess***

AND WHEN WE

PUT OUR FAITH IN

CHRIST . . .

WE CAN REST IN
KNOWING THAT
EVERYTHING IS
ALL RIGHT.

our sins, He is faithful and just [true to His own nature and promises], and will forgive our sins and cleanse us continually from all unrighteousness [our wrongdoing, everything not in conformity with His will and purpose].

If you're worried that you'll just keep sinning because you know God will always forgive you, then you need to understand that when you sincerely give your heart to Him, you won't want to live in sin anymore. Romans 6:1-2 (NIV) says, *. . . Shall we go on sinning so that grace may increase? By no means! We are those who have died to sin; how can we live in it any longer?*

The liberty we have in Christ is never a license to sin; it's complete freedom to be the person God created us to be and fulfill

His plans and purposes for our lives.

I want to encourage you to be determined to live in the freedom Christ died to give you, because there will be times when you have to fight the good fight of faith to hold on to it. Galatians 5:1 (NIV) says, ***It is for freedom that Christ has set us free. Stand firm, then, and do not let yourselves be burdened again by a yoke of slavery.***

JOY COMES THROUGH GOD'S GIFT OF RIGHTEOUSNESS

Just as God's love and forgiveness must be received as gifts, the same is true when it comes to His righteousness. And we must know who we are in Christ—confident that we are right with God—to have peace with ourselves and like ourselves.

Romans 5:9 says we are **justified [declared free of the guilt of sin] by His blood.** And Ephesians 2:8 says, **It is by grace [God's remarkable compassion and favor drawing you to Christ] that you have been saved [actually delivered from judgment and given eternal life] through faith. And this [salvation] is not of yourselves [not through your own effort], but it is the [undeserved, gracious] gift of God.**

So we don't need to wear ourselves out trying to be right with God through our own effort. The truth is, we can't make our lives right on our own, but we can receive the righteousness of God by putting our faith in Christ.

We need to resist the pull of self-righteousness that drives us to make ourselves right with God. Jesus—our Savior—is the only One who can make us righteous before God.

Self-righteousness is believing we are made right with God through our own works. For example, a person might think, *Well, if I read through my Bible every year, then God will be pleased with me.* But the truth is, we don't have to read our Bible to please God; we read it because it helps us in our everyday life. It's for our own good.

In the same way, teaching God's Word doesn't make me a righteous person. The only way we are made righteous (right with God) is by having faith in Jesus Christ—it's not something we can ever earn in our own effort.

I used to really struggle with self-righteousness. I remember a time many years ago when somebody came to the church I was attending and suggested that we all read through the Bible in a year. The pastor got on board, and every Sunday he'd ask, "Who's been doing your Bible reading?" Well, I didn't want to be the one who couldn't raise her hand, so I got really serious about it.

So one day I decided I was going to catch up, and I zipped through the chapters. And honestly, when I closed my Bible I felt so relieved. But then I almost immediately heard the Holy Spirit speak to my heart, "So, tell Me, what did you learn?" And I realized I could not remember one thing!

God taught me an important lesson that day. He would rather we read one verse and actually get something out of it and connect with Him than read 36 chapters and learn nothing. The point is, we need to have the right motives for the things we do and stop making laws out of tasks that make us feel better about ourselves but are unfruitful.

In 2 Corinthians 5:21, we see that Christ took our sin upon Himself so we could become the righteousness of God, entering into a right relationship with Him. This doesn't mean that once we accept Christ we are immediately perfect; no one does everything right all the time. But it does mean we have the Holy Spirit living in us to empower us to do the right things.

God wants us to live through faith in Christ, because then, as we have a personal relationship with Him, we'll do the right thing by His grace because we *want* to do the right thing. He puts the desire in us to do what's right.

In Philippians 3:3, Paul explains that we should ***place no confidence [in what we have or who we are] in the flesh.*** He goes on to say that he obeyed the law without fault, and if any person had a reason to have confidence in himself by the law's standard, he had more of a reason than anyone.

In verses 7 through 9 (NKJV) of that chapter, Paul continues, saying, ***But what things were gain to me, these I have counted loss for Christ. Yet indeed I also count all things loss for the excellence of the knowledge of Christ Jesus my Lord, for whom I have suffered the loss of all things, and count them as rubbish, that I may gain Christ*** *and be found in Him, not having my own righteousness, which is from the law, but that which is through faith in Christ, the righteousness which is from God by faith.*

Paul is saying in order to have a relationship with Christ, he had to be willing to gather up all of his accomplishments and the things he had worked so hard for and be willing to get rid of them all. That's because it's nothing but "rubbish" compared to the priceless privilege of knowing Christ as our Lord and Savior.

Yes, what we do matters, but our good works do not make us acceptable to God. We are only made right with Him by putting our faith in Jesus Christ. And when we put our faith in Christ, we can rest in knowing that everything is all right.

NOT ONLY DO WE
NEED TO LOVE
OURSELVES. . . .

BUT WE NEED TO
LOVE OUR LIFE.

CHAPTER THREE

The Joy of Loving Your Life

I don't often recommend a movie, but there is a great message in *The Five People You Meet in Heaven* that illustrates a biblical principle I want to talk about.

This is a movie about a man who felt like his life had been a failure. He saw himself as a failure and believed he hadn't accomplished anything important. When the movie begins, he is up in years, working at an amusement park, and it's the last place in the world he wants to work. His parents had once owned the park, and he always believed his dad had wasted his life, so he never wanted to be like him or do what his dad did.

He once had grand plans to get away and pursue another great life, but because various things happened, he was never able to leave it and move on to something else. Even though he was very unhappy on the inside, it wasn't obvious to people around him. He was actually a very nice man—he helped a lot of people, was generous, would help his coworkers who were having financial troubles—but he still felt like a failure.

Sadly, he died one day while saving a little girl who was nearly killed on one of the amusement park rides. He went to heaven (keep in mind this is a fictional story, so some details aren't biblically accurate) and when he got there, he was told that he would meet five people who would help him make his decision about what he wanted his heaven to be like.

In this story, everybody who went to heaven was able to choose what they wanted their own heaven to be like. If you wanted it to be an island in Hawaii, then you could live on the beach. If you wanted to live in the Swiss Alps, you could have that environment. Each person could create his own existence.

The decision-making process involved meeting five people, and at first, he didn't understand what was going on. He met a man he had served with in the Vietnam War and learned he had saved his life. His buddy told him what he had meant to him and what he had gone on to accomplish in his own life. Then he met a little girl who he snatched from an oncoming car, saving her life, and learned what she had gone on to do. Throughout the movie, five different people came to him, and each one told a similar story.

In the end, Eddie realizes his life did have meaning and purpose. After meeting the fifth person, a young girl named Tala, he sees that even during his time working at the amusement park, he helped protect children who visited the park from potential dangers. He is then able to have peace about the life he lived, and he chooses the amusement park to be his heaven.

LOVE YOURSELF
LOVE YOUR LIFE

This movie's message is so important: Not only do we need to love ourselves, but we need to love our life. We need to stop wanting someone else's life. Stop wanting to look like someone else or have someone else's gifts and talents. We need to embrace our life and realize the real satisfaction in life is often found in <u>the little things</u>.

If you embrace this lesson and contemplate it, it can be life-changing for you because it will make the difference between enjoying your everyday life or just getting through it. Instead of going through your life always wishing for something you don't have, make the most of what you have right now. Be a blessing right where you are. Be the best "you" that you can be—right where you are. You can be assured, if God wants you somewhere else, He'll put you there.

God can open doors of opportunity that no one else can open, and He always has your best interest in mind. But the best way you can honor God is to be thankful for the life you have and trust Him to bring the right changes at the right times.

I know this is true because I have lived it. It's not about how much money you have or what kind of house you have. It's not about your position at work, your social status, or your position at church. You know something? There are only a handful of people who everyone sees and admires. Most people believe they are just plain, common folks in their little world, doing their little thing. The devil loves to make us think we're nothing. But our lives, our choices, are the stuff life is made of.

I have spent many years behind podiums, speaking to large audiences all over the world, but that does not make up the majority of my life. If I only get excited about being on a platform, speaking to crowds, then I'll miss out on the purpose God has for me in the rest of it. I'll waste much of my life and miss out on many opportunities to show His love and be a blessing to others.

I'm a person with a husband, children and grandchildren. I go through the same kinds of struggles in this world that you have to face. I've learned it's not what I do behind the podium that's the most important to God, it's what I do behind closed doors at home.

It's how I treat people in the marketplace and people who are in need, and what kind of giver I am in my everyday life.

And I don't want to waste a single moment of the life Jesus died to give me!

AND AS WE ARE

OBEDIENT TO

GOD . . .

WE WILL SHOW
OTHERS HOW
TO SEEK GOD'S
JUSTICE.

REFUSE TO WASTE THE LIFE GOD HAS GIVEN YOU

The character in *The Five People You Meet in Heaven* hated his life, and he wasted much of it because he seldom enjoyed it. This is such a tragedy, and we need to learn this lesson so we won't make the same mistake.

If we're going to get the most out of the life Jesus died to give us, we need to keep our focus on God, and strive to be thankful for every good thing He's given us. We need to stay sensitive to the Holy Spirit so we can follow His lead and not miss opportunities right in front of us to help others.

I want to encourage you to be determined to refuse to live with a negative, discouraged attitude or let worry and reasoning suck the life out of you. Do what you can do in each situation and trust God to take care of the things you can't do anything about.

> *Do what you can, and trust*
> *God to do what you can't.*

We also need to know our main purpose, and our specific purpose, in life. Our main purpose is to worship and revere God, to know Him and to obey Him. In Ecclesiastes 12:13, Solomon says it so beautifully: **When all has been heard, the end of the matter is: fear God [worship Him with awe-filled reverence, knowing that He is almighty God] and keep His commandments . . . .**

By the time Solomon wrote those words, he had tried everything—women, money, wealth—yet none of those things had given him lasting happiness. After all of it he said, "Here's the end of the matter: Fear God." God calls us to relieve the oppressed and correct the oppressor, to defend the fatherless, and plead for the widow. And as we are obedient to God, we will show others how to seek God's justice.

We need to have a reverential fear of God. We need to know that God is God and that He means business. He's not just our buddy—He's God Almighty, God All-powerful, All-knowing and entirely good. God sees everything. He knows everything. Just because we go home and close the door so our Bible study friends can't see, it doesn't mean God doesn't see us.

We know we're living with the fear of the Lord when we start living before God to the point where we willingly do everything for the Lord—not to get a pat on the back or applause from people.

Colossians 3:23 (NIV) says, ***Whatever you do, work at it with all your heart, as working for the Lord, not for human masters.*** We should live for the Lord in every area of our lives, because we love Him and know His eye is always on us.

The Bible says the beginning of wisdom is the fear of God (see Proverbs 9:10). When we get a revelation of who God is—that He's omnipotent, omniscient and omnipresent —then we have a reverential fear, or awe, of Him. We are humbled before Him, and we will worship Him—the ever-present, all knowing, all-seeing, all-powerful, almighty, and everlasting God. He loves you, and He has commanded you to love yourself *and* your life.

God wants us to take the free gift of His love and let it heal our wounded souls so we can be about His business—loving other people.

WE OFTEN
THINK WE NEED
SOMEONE TO
LOVE US . . .

BUT WHAT WE

REALLY NEED

IS SOMEONE

TO LOVE.

CHAPTER FOUR

*Loving Your Neighbor
As You Love Yourself*

While our main purpose in life is to worship God ... to have a relationship with Him, receive His love, and love Him ... our specific purpose in this world is lived out as we follow the two greatest commandments He's given us.

In John 13:34-35 (AMPC), Jesus says, ***I give you a new commandment: that you should love one another. Just as I have loved you, so you too should love one another. By this shall all [men] know that you are My disciples, if you love one another [if you keep on showing love among yourselves].***

Matthew 22:37-38 says, *. . . **You shall love
the Lord your God with all your heart and
with all your soul and with all your mind
(intellect). This is the . . . first commandment.
And a second is like it: You shall love your
neighbor as [you do] yourself*** (AMPC).

The love message is the power of the
Gospel. It's so simple: Love God and love
your neighbor as you love yourself. We often
think we need someone to love us, but what
we really need is someone to love. And the
world is desperate for real love, so it isn't
hard to find someone who needs to be loved.

It's important for us to understand that
we can't give away what we don't have,
so we need to spend time developing our
relationship with God, receiving His love
before we try to give His love away.

I remember when God revealed to me that I needed to receive His love so the wounds in my soul could be healed and I could have a healthy relationship with myself. I decided to study God's love in the Word, pray for God to change my heart, and confess what His Word says about His love for me. Every day I would say out loud, "God loves me," and I would say it over and over to purposely keep this truth in my heart throughout the day. After a year of doing this, I finally got a revelation about God's love for me.

Now I am able to receive God's love and love others the way Jesus taught us to love. I don't do it perfectly all the time, but I've come a long way and am making progress every day. My prayer is, "God, show me how I can help others. Make me a blessing everywhere I go. I want to live to love You and others."

The transformation in my soul has been life-changing, and it's given me the ability to do what I'm doing in ministry today. The same priniciple is true for you. I want to encourage you to let God work in your heart and develop godly character in your soul so you can live out the commandments He's given us to love others.

OBEDIENCE TO GOD DEVELOPS GODLY CHARACTER

I believe the greatest miracle of all happens when God changes a person's heart and character to be more like Christ—to be a new creation in Christ (see 2 Corinthians 5:17). Character is developed through our everyday life experiences, and we develop godly character as we learn how to be obedient to God.

Our world is in a state of moral decline; there is so much turmoil in people's lives today . . . so much darkness. People are looking for real hope, and as Christians, we can help them find what they need through a personal relationship with Jesus. We can show them the peace, joy, fulfillment and satisfaction that only comes through living a holy life.

Holiness is what makes us different than those who don't know Christ. When I say "holiness," I'm talking about behavior that's borne out of a personal, intimate relationship with God. It's a place of consecration that causes us to be obedient to the Holy Spirit in our everyday lives, walking in love toward others, looking for ways to help the hurting.

It's about *being* like Christ, not doing good

works to earn God's love or try to alleviate guilt or shame in our souls.

THE PURSUIT OF HOLINESS

Hebrews 12:14 tells us to pursue holiness. Different Bible versions use words like "work at," "make every effort," "strive," and "*be*." Holiness is the outcome of a work of consecration that God does in each of us through our personal relationship with Him. It begins the moment we receive Christ as our Savior.

When He comes to live in our heart, we are made holy at that moment. And then little by little, or from glory to glory, He changes us from the inside out so we become more and more like Him (see 2 Corinthians 3:18).

This pursuit is a process by which we are broken and humbled. We learn how to cooperate with God in this work. We learn to lay down our pride and selfishness. We learn to forget ourselves, and in obedience to the Holy Spirit, live to be a blessing to others. We go from, "What about me?" to "How can I help you?"

Going through this transformation is a process and it takes time. Don't worry if you feel you haven't "arrived." The fact that you are dissatisfied with where you are, or that you're seeking to be a better person, or you're in a place of conviction means you *are* making progress. God didn't promise the process would be fast . . . or easy . . . or feel good all the time. Just be thankful for His love and grace while He works.

Now, at any point in the process, we can always be a blessing. I like to say bloom where you are planted. We can be good to somebody anytime. We just need to be real…to share our struggles, as well as our victories.

In my personal life, I try to make it my business to add value to everybody I come in contact with. I can honestly say that learning how to love others with God's love has made me the happiest I've ever been. The truth is, you can't be selfish and be happy or have peace.

Make it your goal each day to pursue God's love and then give it away. First Corinthians 14:1 (AMPC) says, ***Eagerly pursue and seek*** *to acquire [this] love [make it your aim, your great quest] . . . .* So go after it with all your might, and ask God to make you a blessing everywhere you go. You can do something to help someone. You can live to love, just like Jesus.

LIVE TO GIVE

Matthew 16:24 (AMPC) says, *Then Jesus said to His disciples, If anyone desires to be My disciple, let him deny himself [disregard, lose sight of, and forget himself and his own interests] and take up his cross and follow Me [cleave steadfastly to Me, conform wholly to My example in living and, if need be, in dying, also].*

This scripture is saying that if you want to

be happy, you have to learn to give your life away, or "live to give." This is not easy in the beginning because we are naturally selfish people, accustomed to thinking about ourselves first. But in order to really live, you have to die to yourself first. I'm not talking about physical death, but being willing to give up what you want all the time to be a blessing to others.

I know what this is like because I used to think I was the center of my universe and I was miserable! But when I learned the truth about what Jesus meant when He said we must deny ourselves, lose sight of our interests, forget about ourselves and take up our cross to follow Him, it was life-changing.

To forget yourself doesn't mean you shouldn't take care of yourself or that you never get to do anything you want to do; it just means you don't have yourself on your mind all the time. And taking up our cross to follow Jesus is all about losing sight of ourselves and our own interests so we can say, "Here I am, God. I give my life to You and I want You to use me in any way that You want to work in and through my life."

I want to encourage you to make a determined decision to fulfill God's commandments to love every day of your life. It won't always be easy, convenient or comfortable, but in those times, remember that God loves you and He always has your best interest at heart, so whatever He shows you to do, it's for your good. And if we trust Him, we'll find that doing things His way, by His grace, leads us to the happiest life we could ever have.

Ephesians 3:17 (AMPC) is a powerful

scripture that I love to pray for others.
It says, **May Christ through your faith [actually] dwell (settle down, abide, make His permanent home) in your hearts! May you be rooted deep in love and founded securely on love.**

This scripture is saying that God loves you; His will is for you to be His child and receive every blessing He has for you—righteousness, peace, joy, provision of your needs, healing and restoration. In Christ, you have a personal relationship with your Father God, and you can hear from God and be led by the Holy Spirit, who lives in your spirit. In Christ, you have access to God's grace and strength to do whatever you need to do. Because of God's grace, you are blessed and you can love Him, love yourself and love others the way God loves you!